ORANGES & LEMONS

ORANGES & LEMONS

HELEN SUDELL

PHOTOGRAPHS BY MICHELLE GARRETT

LORENZ BOOKS

LONDON • NEW YORK • SYDNEY • BATH

This edition published in the UK in 1997 by Lorenz Books

Lorenz Books is an imprint of
Anness Publishing Limited
Hermes House
88–89 Blackfriars Road
London SE1 8HA

This edition published in Canada by Lorenz Books, distributed by
Raincoast Books Distribution Limited, Vancouver

© 1997 Anness Publishing Limited

ISBN 1 85967 338 4

British cataloguing-in data available from the British Library

Publisher: Joanna Lorenz
Managing Editor: Helen Sudell
Introduction by: Beverley Jollands
Designer: Lilian Lindblom
Photographer: Michelle Garrett
Step photography: Janine Hosegood
Illustrator: Lucinda Ganderton

Printed in China

1 3 5 7 9 10 8 6 4 2

CONTENTS

INTRODUCTION

A deep blue sky, intense sunshine, clear colours throbbing in Mediterranean light, deep green leaves: these create the perfect setting for vibrant, fragrant oranges and lemons, fruits glowing with health and liveliness. Paradoxically at their best during the cold northern winter, they are like little parcels of liquid summer. The colours of their smooth yet textured skins – zingiest orange, the most acid of yellows – are an apt visual match for their wide-awake flavours.

Like many other exotics, oranges and lemons were introduced to Europe by Arab traders. The orange's name comes from the ancient Indian word *narayam*, which means "perfume within" and seems an unbeatable description of the magical fruit we all now take for granted. Conquering Muslim armies in the seventh century spread the cultivation of oranges, tangerines and lemons through the Mediterranean to Spain, where the courtyards of the Great Mosque at Cordoba and at the Alhambra in Granada were filled with citrus trees. Oranges were always desirable and a sign of wealth: the tables of the medieval rich groaned with orange-flavoured dishes, and the flowers were distilled to make scent.

The arms of the incredibly wealthy and powerful Medici family included five orange balls – were these indeed oranges? Whatever their origin, the artists who enjoyed the patronage of the Medicis exploited the resemblance and introduced the picturesque fruit into their paintings as subtle compliments to their benefactors. There are orange trees peeping over the wall behind the Virgin and Child in an altarpiece by Domenico Veneziano and they form the tapestried backdrop to Botticelli's *Primavera*.

In colder climates, where orange and lemon trees couldn't be planted outside, the difficulties of cultivating them raised their status even higher: they had to be grown in pots. These weren't little plants, however, they were serious trees. They needed skilled gardeners to look after them and a substantial building to house them in winter. So orangeries became another good way of showing off fabulous wealth. Louis XIV's orangery at Versailles was the ultimate

status symbol. In England, Queen Henrietta Maria's orangery at Wimbledon contained 42 orange trees and one fruit-bearing lemon tree. Others were built at Chiswick House, Hampton Court, Kensington Palace and Kew. The orangeries were light, airy, decorative, fragrant – above all, impressive – places to take guests for a stroll on a chilly day. When the frosts had passed, the trees could be taken outside by a small army of servants: "Some keep them in great square boxes, and lift them to and fro by iron hooks on the sides, or cause them to be rowled by trundles, or small wheels under them..." wrote John Parkinson in 1629.

Having to grow the trees in pots only adds to their prettiness: they have the lovely habit of flowering and fruiting simultaneously, and their strong colours and shiny dark leaves offsetting the delicate flowers look even more beautiful when set in a deep blue box or an elegant urn: all in all,

Above: Angelic cherubs play in an orange tree on this sixteenth-century decorative screen.

they are a designer's dream. Lord Leighton's voluptuous painting of *The Garden of the Hesperides* takes advantage of the theory that the mythical golden apples were really oranges, and his curvaceous nymphs loll under a huge potted orange tree drooping with heavy fruit. The Victorian designer William de Morgan was equally inspired by

Above: A late sixteenth-century cushion cover embroidered with silk and silver thread. Note the orange and lemon trees around the huntsmen.

the sensuality of the warm south, and painted Italianate tile panels of potted citrus trees. Victorian decorators of the 1880s could combine these with William Morris's wallpaper design "Fruit" in which lemons dangled from

flowery branches. Encapsulating all the elements of rarity, jewel-like brilliance and an ornamental shape, one of the imperial Easter eggs created by Fabergé contained a miniature orange tree, from amongst whose jade leaves and jewelled fruit sprang a minute clockwork singing bird.

The hot colours and graphic shapes of citrus fruit were bound to appeal to twentieth-century designers. They suited the style of Clarice Cliff perfectly, and designs for her Bizarre range of ceramics in the early thirties included three popular patterns called "Delecia Citrus", "Oranges" and "Oranges and Lemons". Also much sought-after today, Carlton produced tableware in the shape of fruit, including an orange-shaped marmalade jar and a dish shaped like a lemon, with pitted surfaces that imitated the texture of the peel. Fifties textile designs exploited the shapes of the whole fruit and also the wheel-like pattern inside.

You can use all these elements in designs for your own home. You can also, of course,

just use the fruit itself: a bowl of oranges or lemons provides an instant colour accent in a room, and clementines still attached to their leafy stems are as welcome on the Christmas table for their looks as for their flavour. In recent seasons there has been a welcome move away from gaudy Christmas decorations and a return to real foliage and a more natural, restrained style: dried slices of orange and lemon or home-made pomanders are perfect to hang on the Christmas tree with other pretty natural ornaments like pine cones and bunches of cinnamon sticks, and all add the extra dimension of scent to your decorations.

Lots of the designs that follow would look great in a sunny conservatory – think of the

Top: An early twentieth-century biscuit tin decorated with an orange and lemon border motif.

Above: A mosaic of citrus fruits and leaves found in Pompeii, Italy.

old orangeries – or, naturally, in the kitchen, especially now that kitchen designs are glowing again with bright, clear colours. Pick up on the strong design qualities of these fruits – their shapes, textures, colours – and fill your home with summer brightness.

Above: A late nineteenth-century tapestry by William Morris, showing orange and apple trees in an imaginary orchard.

PINPRICKED FRUIT LAMPSHADE

This is a satisfying way to turn a plain paper lampshade into something special. Switching on the light transforms the delicate pricked design into a magical pattern of stars.

YOU WILL NEED

MATERIALS
purchased paper lampshade

EQUIPMENT
tracing paper
pencil
paper for templates
scissors
masking tape
towel
darning needle
cork (optional)
thimble (optional)

1 Trace the templates at the back of the book and enlarge them if necessary to suit the size of the lampshade. Copy them several times and cut out roughly.

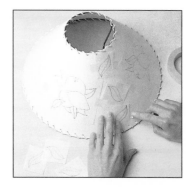

2 Arrange the motifs in a repeating pattern on the outside of the lampshade and secure with masking tape. Trace the shape of the stuck-on motifs on the inside of the shade.

3 Rest the lampshade on a towel and, working from the inside of the shade, gently pierce the design with a darning needle. You can bind the needle with masking tape or stick it into a cork to make it easier to hold – alternatively use a thimble. Finish the design with a scalloped edging.

MEXICAN PAINTED CITRUS TRAY

Breakfast in bed will really wake you up if it is presented on this flamboyant tray. The bold fruit motif, painted in zingy, sunny colours, is full of the energy and simplicity of folk art.

YOU WILL NEED

MATERIALS
wooden tray
matt emulsion paint: dark emerald, lime green and turquoise
acrylic gouache paints
matt polyurethane varnish

EQUIPMENT
sandpaper
medium and fine paintbrushes
tracing paper
soft and hard pencils
masking tape

1 Sand the tray to remove any varnish. Paint the whole tray a dark emerald green colour, then paint the inside of the tray in lime green, and the base with turquoise. Leave to dry.

2 Trace the motifs at the back of the book for the base and outer sides of the tray. Rub over the outlines on the reverse of the tracing with a soft pencil, then transfer the designs.

3 Paint the oranges, lemons and leaves on the base of the tray, and the flower motif on the outer sides, using acrylic gouache. When dry, add the details in white.

4 Paint a pink wavy border around the edge and the base of the tray. Paint the handle holes in bright orange. When the paint is dry, protect with several coats of varnish.

ORANGE-TREE NOTEBOOK COVER

Stitch a delicate appliquéd cover for a special diary, address book or birthday book. The little tree, with its button oranges, would be particularly appropriate for a gardening or cookery notebook.

1 Cut a rectangle of cream fabric slightly smaller than the front of your notebook. Scale up the template at the back of the book so that it will fit this neatly. Trace the shapes on to the backing paper of the fusible bonding web and cut out roughly. Iron the pieces on to their respective fabrics, then cut out.

2 Peel off the backing papers and iron on to the cream fabric. Chain stitch around the leaves in green thread. Work the urn handles in orange, and chain stitch around the urn. Cut the fabric for the cover: the width needs to be four times that of the book and the depth 2.5 cm/ 1 in more. Press under a 2.5cm/ 1 in fold at each short edge.

3 Fold in half, wrong sides together, and wrap around the book. Tuck the loose fabric under the front cover and stitch the embroidered panel on the centre front. Fold the flaps under the book covers and loosely tack the raw edges together at top and bottom. Slip the cover off and machine stitch along the tacked lines. Turn the cover right side out and press. Sew the buttons on to the tree.

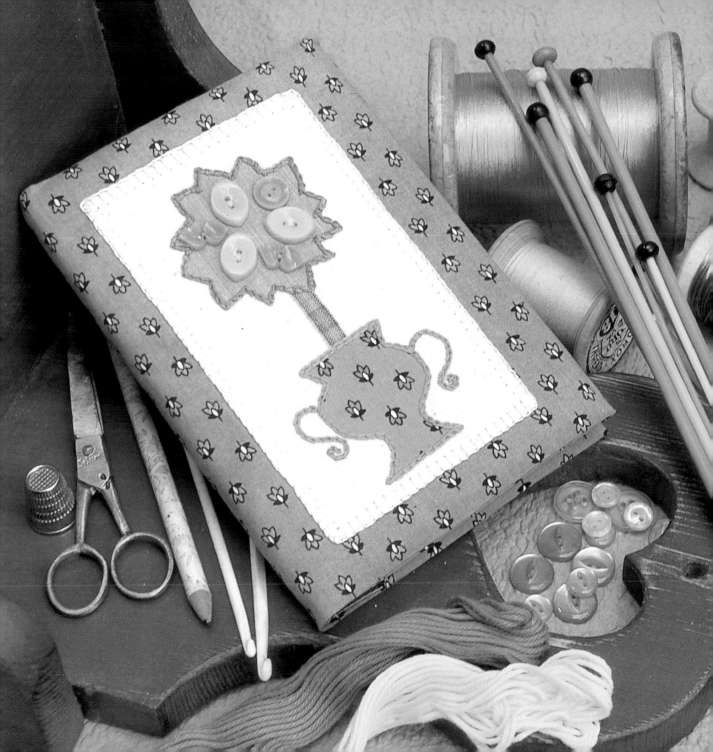

ORANGE-SLICE EARRINGS

B right, jolly earrings to suit the mood of a hot summer's day, or cheer up a dull one. Have fun making the orange slices as realistic as you can – these even have pips.

YOU WILL NEED

MATERIALS
*polymer clay in pearl, pale orange and dark orange
earring findings: earring hooks, large rings and eye pins*

EQUIPMENT
*craft knife
cutting mat
bamboo skewer
rolling pin
old cheese grater
round-nosed pliers*

To assemble each earring: loop the wire extending from the small orange and snip off any excess. Put a large ring through the orange slice and attach to the small orange. Attach the earring hook above the small orange.

1 Roll a 5 mm/¼ in diameter sausage of pearl clay. Roll the pale orange clay into a 1.5 cm/⅝ in diameter sausage and cut it lengthwise into four triangular segments.

3 Roll out a piece of dark orange clay very thinly and cut strips 1 cm/½ in wide to fit between the segments. Arrange the pieces together to make a semicircle. Roll out a 3 mm/⅛ in layer of pearl and a 2 mm/¹⁄₁₂ in layer of dark orange for the peel and mould these around the edge. Make two 1 cm/½ in balls in dark orange and roll on a grater to make them look like small oranges. Fit an eye pin through the centre of each. Trim any overlapping edges from the large orange segment and roll the peel on a grater.

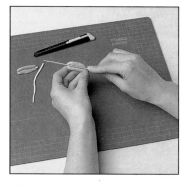

2 Cut lengthwise into two of the triangles and insert a skewer. Press the clay together to form a tunnel. Fill the tunnel with the sausage of pearl clay and reform the triangular shape.

4 Cut two 5 mm/¼ in slices and make a hole in each for the earring finding. Bake all the pieces at 110°C/225°F/Gas ¼ for 20–30 minutes.

ORANGE BOWL

Hoard old magazines so that you can assemble a good collection of orange and yellow papers for this papier-mâché bowl: it is designed to look like half an orange, plain on the outside and textured inside.

YOU WILL NEED

MATERIALS
petroleum jelly
old newspapers, torn into strips
wallpaper paste
old magazine pages which are
  predominantly orange and
  yellow
orange wrapping paper
gloss varnish
gold paint

EQUIPMENT
large bowl to use as mould
scissors
medium and fine paintbrushes

1 Coat the inside of the bowl with petroleum jelly. Soak the newspaper strips in wallpaper paste. Cover the inside of the bowl with at least ten layers of strips. Leave the bowl to dry out completely, then gently ease it from the mould.

3 Cover the outside of the bowl with torn strips of plain orange wrapping paper, carefully overlapping the edges.

2 Tear the magazine pages into long, narrow triangles and paste them around the inside of the bowl so that they taper towards the bottom.

4 Leave the bowl to dry completely, then trim the top edge using scissors. Coat the bowl with a protective layer of varnish. Paint a thin line of gold paint along the top edge to complete the bowl.

CITRUS ROLLER BLIND

Stylized, almost abstract, oranges and lemons on this stencilled blind give it a fifties feel. It would look great in a kitchen decorated with strong, fresh colours.

YOU WILL NEED

MATERIALS
plain white cotton fabric to fit
  window
acrylic gouache paints: orange,
  yellow, lime green, black and
  red
roller blind fabric stiffener
roller blind kit

EQUIPMENT
tracing paper
pencil
stencil card
craft knife
cutting mat
masking tape
scissors
stencil brush
large paintbrush

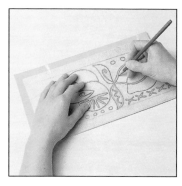

1 Scale up the template at the back of the book so that the repeat design will fit across the width of your blind, and trace it. Transfer it three times on to stencil card. Using a craft knife, cut out only the areas you will need for each stencil:
(1) the lemons, oranges and red spots; (2) the leaves; (3) the black details.

2 Lay out the white fabric on a smooth flat surface and secure with masking tape. Using gouache paints, stencil the oranges and lemons motif all over the fabric. Keep the stencil brush as dry as possible, blotting off excess paint, and clean the stencil if paint starts to bleed under the edges.

3 Leave the orange and lemon motifs to dry, then proceed with the remaining colours. Paint the leaves next, then the red spots (using the first stencil) and finally the black details. When dry, paint the fabric with fabric stiffener following the manufacturer's instructions and hang on a washing line to dry, keeping it very straight. Make up the blind using the blind kit.

FRUITY APPLIQUÉ CUSHION

A bright, graphic cushion which would be ideal for a kitchen, a sunny garden bench or conservatory.

YOU WILL NEED

MATERIALS
orange cotton fabric,
  60 x 15 cm/24 x 6 in
yellow cotton fabric,
  45 x 15 cm/18 x 6 in
green cotton fabric,
  30 x 15 cm/12 x 6 in
matching sewing thread
fusible bonding web
craft felt in orange, yellow and
  four shades of green
blue-and-white check cotton
  fabric, 60 x 90 cm/24 x 36 in
five 2.5 cm/1 in self-cover
  buttons
50 cm/20 in cushion pad

EQUIPMENT
scissors
sewing machine
iron and pressing cloth
tracing paper
pencil
thin card or paper for templates
pins
sewing needle

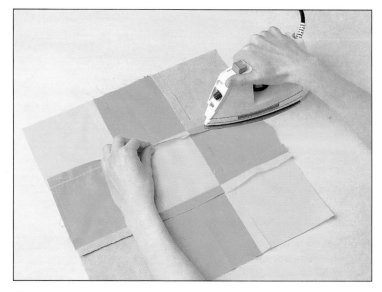

1 Cut the cotton fabric into 15 cm/6 in squares: four orange, three yellow and two green. Machine stitch together in three rows of three, using a 1 cm/½ in seam allowance. Press the seams open. Join the three strips into a square, carefully matching the seams, and press the long seams open.

2 Enlarge the templates at the back of the book and then trace the fruit and leaf shapes on to the backing paper of the fusible bonding web. Cut the shapes out roughly and iron on to the different coloured felts, then cut out accurately along the outlines.

3 Peel off the paper backing and place the shapes on the coloured squares, arranging the leaves so that they lie under the orange and yellow circles. Iron them in place using a pressing cloth and following the bonding web manufacturer's instructions.

4 Trace the shapes for the second layer of appliqué shapes – the orange slices, leaf veins and the star-shaped trim for the whole oranges – on to the bonding web. Then cut out from felt just as before and press in place.

5 From the check fabric cut two rectangles 53 x 45 cm/ 21 x 18 in and two strips 8 x 40 cm/3¼ x 16 in. Sew the two strips along opposite sides of the appliqué square. Turn under and stitch a double hem along one long side of each large rectangle. Make five evenly spaced buttonholes along one hemmed edge, then, with the right sides facing, sew the unfinished long edges to the remaining two sides of the square.

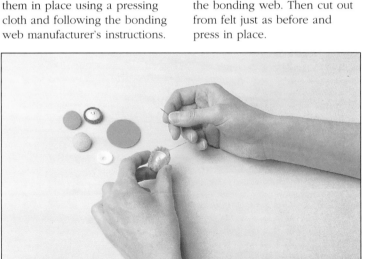

6 Following the button manufacturer's instructions, cover each of the five buttons in a different coloured felt.

7 Fold the two back panels to the wrong side, leaving a 6 cm/2½ in check border at the front of the cushion cover. Pin and then stitch the seams, leaving a 1 cm/½ in seam allowance. Turn to the right side and press. Sew the buttons in place. Insert the cushion pad and do up the buttons.

PUNCHED TIN CITRUS DOOR PANEL

Traditional tin-punching is a satisfying and stylish way to transform a plain panelled door. The strong graphic outline of the lemon and orange slices and the pitted texture of the peel make the fruits very appropriate motifs for this treatment.

YOU WILL NEED

MATERIALS
small cupboard with panelled door
3 mm/⅛ in tin sheet to fit inside door panel
strong clear glue

EQUIPMENT
tracing paper
pencil
scissors
cardboard
masking tape
hammer
steel punch

1 Scale up the template at the back of the book to fit the size of your door panel, and trace on to tracing paper. Lay the tin sheet on a piece of cardboard and attach the traced design using masking tape.

2 Starting with the square boxes around the fruit, hammer the steel punch every 2 mm/1⁄12 in to make a small dent. Hammer the larger dents to either side of the centre lines. Hammer small dents along all the fruit and leaf outlines.

3 Remove the tracing paper and fill in the whole fruit shapes with dents. Fill in the outer rims of the lemon slices with small dents.

4 Spread strong glue over the back of the tin and on the cupboard panel. Leave until tacky, then glue in position.

LEMON TILES

You could paint this fresh, graphic design on individual tiles to make focal points on the wall or create a repeating design by setting decorated tiles in groups or rows. Reserve some tiles to paint with a simple "filler" design like the checks used here. Use solvent-based ceramic paints that do not need to be fired.

YOU WILL NEED

MATERIALS
plain white ceramic tiles
ceramic paints
transparent ceramic paint
  medium

EQUIPMENT
tracing paper
pencil
ruler
paper for template
scissors
carbon paper
masking tape
paintbrush

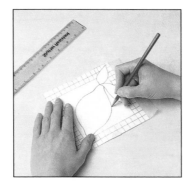

1 Enlarge the template at the back of the book so that it fits the tiles exactly and copy all the outlines of the design. Decorate the border with squares if required.

2 Place a sheet of carbon paper on the tile, then the paper template, and secure with masking tape. Draw over the outlines with a sharp pencil to transfer the design.

3 Mix up enough ceramic paint in each colour to complete all the tiles you need, adding ceramic paint medium to give transparency. Paint the tile, allowing each colour to dry before applying the next.

ORANGE BASKET SAMPLER

The fruit basket, piled high with oranges and lemons, was a popular cross-stitch motif in the nineteenth century. DMC threads were used in this project but it is easy to match the colours from any other thread manufacturer.

YOU WILL NEED

MATERIALS
14-count white Aida cloth,
15 x 20 cm (6 x 8 in)
stranded embroidery thread,
1 skein each of orange,
light orange, yellow, ochre,
dark olive, light olive and
chocolate brown
mount board
plain wooden frame with
9 x 14 cm (3½ x 5½ in)
opening

EQUIPMENT
tacking thread
sewing needle
tapestry needle
embroiderer's scissors
iron
craft knife
cutting mat

1 Using tacking thread, mark guidelines vertically and horizontally across the centre of the Aida. Following the chart at the back of the book, the sampler is worked with three strands of embroidery thread throughout, and one square of the chart represents one cross stitch. Using orange thread, work the centre orange of the bottom row of fruit.

2 Stitch the other oranges, then work the leaves around them and the basket. Use the guidelines to establish the position of the other motifs and count the squares between them carefully. When the design is complete unpick the tacking threads and press lightly from the back of the work.

3 Cut a piece of mount board to fit the finished piece, using the lining paper from the frame as a guide. Place the board centrally on the back of the work and lace the two long sides together using long stitches. Repeat the process with the two short sides, then insert in the frame.

FRUITY BRACELET

Paint a summery papier-mâché bracelet with oranges and lemons. This one is decorated with slices of different citrus fruits. Making paper pulp is easy: just mix three parts thick wallpaper paste with one part PVA glue. Tear some newspaper into small strips and soak them in the paste.

YOU WILL NEED

MATERIALS
thin cardboard
large hook and eye
masking tape
wallpaper paste
PVA glue
newspaper
strong clear glue
gold foil (from a chocolate wrapper)
acrylic paints: white, yellow, red and orange
gold paint
clear gloss varnish

EQUIPMENT
tracing paper
pencil
scissors
large mixing bowl
paintbrushes

1 Copy the template at the back of the book, enlarge to fit wrist and cut out of thin cardboard. Tape a large hook and eye to either end.

3 Prime the outside of the bracelet with a coat of white acrylic paint to smooth the surface. Decorate with slices of citrus fruit using acrylics. Add touches of gold paint around the edges, pips and dimples.

2 Cover the cardboard with several layers of paper pulp, making sure the masking tape and all the edges are neatly covered. Leave to dry completely. Use strong, clear glue to stick a sheet of gold foil to the inside of the bracelet. Trim the edges.

4 When the paint is dry, protect with clear gloss varnish.

ORANGES & LEMONS TEA TOWEL

Appliquéd shapes and machine embroidery make a hard-wearing decoration for bright tea towels. Choose a strong base shade to match your own kitchen colour scheme, or use these motifs on a set of towels in different colours.

YOU WILL NEED

MATERIALS
fusible bonding web
scraps of cotton fabric in yellow, orange and green
ready-made tea towel
machine embroidery thread in black

EQUIPMENT
tracing paper
pencil
thin card or paper for template
scissors
iron
tailor's chalk
embroidery hoop
sewing machine
sewing needle

1 Copy the template at the back of the book and transfer to thin card or paper. Cut out the orange and lemon motifs. Draw around each motif several times on the paper backing of a piece of fusible bonding web. Cut out roughly. Iron the web on to the wrong side of the fabric scraps and cut neatly around the outlines.

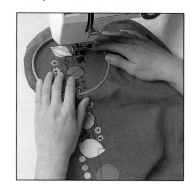

2 Arrange the shapes along the bottom of both ends of the tea towel until you are happy with your design. Remove the paper backing from the fusible bonding web and iron the motifs on to the towel, following the manufacturer's instructions.

3 Use tailor's chalk to join up the motifs with a series of parallel lines. Put the work in an embroidery hoop. Select the darning or free embroidery mode on the sewing machine and attach a darning foot. Using black thread, work several lines of stitching around each fruit and work down the chalk lines with a series of small embroidered motifs. Hand sew French knots on the oranges.

SALT DOUGH FRUIT BASKET

Make this delightful wall decoration from simple ingredients you are bound to have in your kitchen already. Salt dough is quite durable once it is varnished, but remember not to hang it anywhere damp or steamy as this may make it crumble.

YOU WILL NEED

MATERIALS
15 ml/1 tbsp oil
225 g/8 oz flour
225 g/8 oz salt
warm water
paper bowl
paperclip
aluminium foil
4 cloves
acrylic paints
polyurethane satin varnish

EQUIPMENT
mixing bowl
airtight container
rolling pin
small, sharp knife
fork
baking parchment
cheese grater
heart-shaped pastry cutter
baking tray
paintbrushes

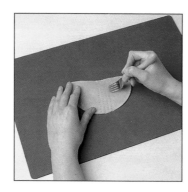

1 To make the salt dough, add the oil to the flour and salt in a mixing bowl and mix to a smooth, stiff dough with warm water. Knead for 10 minutes. For best results, leave to rest overnight in an airtight container. Roll out half the dough to a thickness of 5 mm/ ¼ in. Cut out a large oval and a half oval. Mark a basket pattern on the dough with a fork.

2 Cut the paper bowl in half and trim so that it fits on the large oval. Place the half oval of dough on top of the bowl, moisten the edges and stick to the large oval. Cut 2 cm/¾ in slits along the rim for the ribbon.

3 Use a thinly rolled piece of dough to attach a paperclip to the top of the basket on the reverse side.

4 Roll out two long thin sausages of dough to fit down the side of the basket. Twist them together, moisten the surfaces and stick them to the edge. Make another twist for the other side. Trim and join invisibly at the top and overlap in a "knot" at the bottom of the basket. Make a smaller twisted length for the handle at the top.

5 Roll four walnut-sized balls of aluminium foil. Mould some dough over the foil and make two lemon shapes and two oranges. Roll the fruit over a fine grater to simulate the texture of the skin, and insert a clove at the top. Arrange the fruit inside the basket.

6 Roll out the remaining dough thinly. Cut small rectangles to fit between the slits to look like ribbon. Cut out four heart shapes and then cut them in half and trim to make leaves. Mark the veins with the point of the knife and shape them. Moisten them and arrange around the fruit. Transfer the basket, on the baking parchment, to a baking tray and bake at 120°C/250°F/Gas ½, for 8 hours, or until the basket is completely hardened all over. Allow it to cool.

7 Paint the fruit with acrylic paints. Thin the green paint slightly and paint the leaves. Brush off some of the paint with a stiff, dry brush to add highlights. Paint the ribbon white, allow to dry thoroughly, then paint in a gingham pattern with yellow, orange and green stripes.

8 Paint the basket with a thin wash of burnt sienna mixed with a little black paint. Brush off the excess with a dry brush. Paint the completed basket with at least two coats of polyurethane satin varnish.

SPONGE-PRINTED FRUIT SHELF-EDGING

Shelf-edgings are a lovely decorative detail for a country-style kitchen or breakfast room. Even if you do not possess the perfect heirloom dresser, you can make the plainest of shelves beautiful this way.

YOU WILL NEED

MATERIALS
13 cm/5 in strip unbleached calico the length of your shelf
spray fabric stiffener
fabric paints in red, yellow and green
6 cm/2½ in strip green print cotton fabric the length of your shelf
matching sewing thread
double-sided tape

EQUIPMENT
tracing paper
pencil
thin card or paper for template
scissors
sponge
felt-tipped pen
ruler
paintbrush
iron
pins
sewing machine
sewing needle

1 Enlarge the template at the back of the book so that the triangular shape measures 13 cm/5 in across. Transfer the fruit and leaf outlines to thin card or paper and cut out. Draw around them on to the sponge and cut out the shapes.

3 Stipple darker areas on the fruit and leaves with a paintbrush to give them a three-dimensional look.

2 Mark a row of triangles along one edge of the calico strip. Spray the strip with fabric stiffener and leave to dry, then cut along the pencil lines. Use the sponge blocks to print the fruit design. Print a leaf on each side of the fruit.

4 With wrong sides facing, press the green print fabric in half lengthwise, then press under 5 mm/¼ in along one long edge. With right sides facing, sew the other raw edge to the top of the finished shelf edging with a seam allowance of 5 mm/¼ in. Fold the green fabric over to cover the top and slip stitch the folded edge to the back of the seam. Neaten the corners. Attach to the shelf using double-sided tape.

LEMON SLICE TABLE NAPKIN

These lovely yellow napkins embroidered with cool lemon slices would look delightful on a table set for a summer lunch in the garden.

YOU WILL NEED

MATERIALS
large yellow napkin
embroidery thread in dark and
*   pale yellow, off-white and*
*   dark green*

EQUIPMENT
tracing paper
soft and hard pencils
pins
embroidery needle
iron

1 Trace the template at the back of the book and rub over the lemon motif on the reverse of the tracing with a soft pencil. Pin the tracing in the corner of the napkin and transfer the motif.

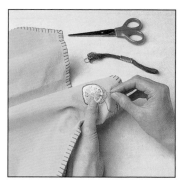

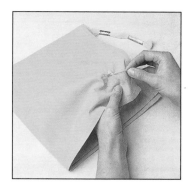

2 Using dark yellow thread, work French knots in the centre of the lemon. Fill the segments in stem stitch using pale yellow. Fill the pith in stem stitch using off-white, and fill the skin area with dark yellow French knots.

3 Work dark green blanket stitch around the hem of the napkin. The stitches can be worked over the existing machine stitching. Work a row of dark yellow stem stitch around the edge of the lemon pith and another row outside that in green. Work a dark green running stitch around the edge of the French knots and add some small dark green stitches as shading in the segments to complete the design. Press the embroidery on the reverse side.

LEMON TREE

This tiny ornamental tree will perfume your room with the invigorating aroma of lemons. When the scent has gradually faded you can refresh it with a few more drops of lemon oil.

YOU WILL NEED

MATERIALS
florist's medium stub wires
brown florist's tape
self-hardening modelling clay
yellow acrylic paint
fine brass wire
green crêpe paper
thin cardboard
PVA glue
4 small wooden beads
dark green gloss paint
sand or gravel
cotton wool
pure lemon oil
orange and lemon peel

EQUIPMENT
wire cutters or old scissors
paintbrushes
tracing paper
pencil
scissors

1 Trim 15 pieces of stub wire to a length of 23 cm/9 in. Bind them all together with brown florist's tape for the first 12 cm/4¾ in, then bind each projecting end in turn. Divide the wires into pairs, and bind each pair part way up. Bend them out from the trunk, then inwards to shape the tree.

3 Trace the template for the box at the back of the book, enlarge to size required and transfer on to thin cardboard. Make up the box by folding along the dotted lines. Glue together and glue a small bead to each corner. Paint the box with dark green gloss paint. Make a narrow cardboard tube to fit the tree trunk and glue into the centre of the box. Fill the box with sand or gravel and top with cotton wool.

2 Make tiny lemons from clay, spike them on to wire and paint yellow. When dry, replace the wire supports with a loop of fine brass wire, covering the join with green crêpe paper.

4 Cut the leaves out of green crêpe paper. Attach the lemons and leaves to the branches. Drip lemon oil on to the cotton wool and cover with orange and lemon peel.

GILDED FRUITS GLASS BOWL

The colours of the fruit really glow in transparent glass paints. Relief gold outliner defines the design like the leading in a stained-glass window. If you have not tried painting on glass before, spend a little time practising the techniques on an old jam jar.

YOU WILL NEED

MATERIALS
glass bowl
gold glass-painting outliner
solvent-based glass paints: red,
  green, yellow

EQUIPMENT
hot, soapy water
tea towel
methylated spirit
kitchen paper
packing material or bean-bag
paintbrushes

1 Wash the bowl in hot, soapy water and dry thoroughly. Wipe over the surface with methylated spirit to remove any remaining traces of grease.

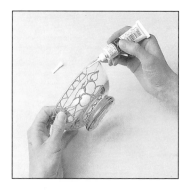

2 After a few practice runs, draw the design carefully with the gold outliner. It is easiest to do this in sections, leaving each section to dry for at least 12 hours before moving on to the next.

3 Prop the bowl on its side, supported by packing material to keep the section that you are painting horizontal so that the paint does not run. Apply the glass paint thickly to avoid streaky brush strokes.

4 Leave each section to dry overnight before beginning the next. If you are a beginner stick to single blocks of colour. More experienced glass painters could try blending two or more colours into each other to achieve an attractive effect.

DÉCOUPAGE LEMON MIRROR FRAME

Hunt around for interesting printed material to combine with the lemon motif on this striking papier-mâché frame. You could use a photocopier to reproduce graphics from books, or you could produce an ancient manuscript of your own!

YOU WILL NEED

MATERIALS
corrugated cardboard
mirror, 15 x 18 cm/6 x 7 in
wallpaper paste
newspaper
acrylic paints: black, yellow and green
paperclip
acrylic gesso
lemon motif wrapping paper
scraps of printed paper or manuscript
white tissue paper
matt acrylic varnish

EQUIPMENT
craft knife
metal ruler
cutting mat
mixing bowl
paintbrush
natural sponge

1 Cut two 17 x 20 cm/ 6½ x 8 in rectangles from the cardboard. Lay the mirror centrally on one piece and cut strips of card to fit around it down two sides and across the bottom. Cut a window out of the centre of the other rectangle of cardboard, leaving a 4 cm/ 1½ in border.

2 Coat all the pieces of cardboard with wallpaper paste; leave to dry. Tear the newspaper into strips and coat with paste. Cover the front of the frame. Paste the spacer strips in position on the sides and bottom of the back panel; cover with papier-mâché strips; leave to dry. Apply a second layer.

3 When the papier-mâché is dry, paint the inside surfaces of the frame black to minimize any possible reflection they might give in the mirror.

4 Open out the paperclip and thread one end through the papier-mâché at the centre back of the frame. Paste strips of newspaper over the clip, leaving the top section showing to act as a hook.

5 Join the front of the frame to the back with more strips of pasted newspaper. Paste folded strips over the top of the frame to either side of the opening for added strength. Once dry, paint the frame with acrylic gesso.

6 Sponge the entire frame with thin yellow paint, then with green paint to create an all-over mottled effect.

7 Tear the lemon motifs from the wrapping paper in interesting shapes and then arrange over the frame. Fill the gaps between the lemons with small pieces of printed paper. Paste in position.

8 To soften the design, tear small pieces of white tissue paper and paste on to the frame, crinkling them slightly and overlapping the edges of some of the motifs. When the paste is dry paint the frame with two coats of matt varnish and insert the mirror into the top slit to finish.

FRUIT TREE TABLE DECORATIONS

Exploit the pitted texture of orange and lemon rind in these pretty foil decorations: make a selection of whole fruit, as well as an ornamental tree in a tub. These exotic table decorations will look lovely underneath a glass bowl or hanging from drinks glasses.

YOU WILL NEED

MATERIALS
PVA glue
aluminium foil
coloured varnish, or clear
  varnish tinted with artist's oil
  colours
fine wire

EQUIPMENT
tracing paper
pencil
dried-out ballpoint pen
old scissors
fine paintbrush

1 Trace the templates at the back of the book. Glue two sheets of aluminium foil together, shiny sides outwards. Lay the tracing over the foil and use a dried-out ballpoint pen to draw around the outlines.

2 Cut out the foil shapes using old scissors, then cover with another sheet of tracing paper to protect the foil. Indent the details on the fruit and leaves with the dried-out ballpoint pen.

3 Using a fine paintbrush, paint the foil shapes with coloured varnish. Leave to dry.

4 Crease the leaves along their central veins and wind the stems around a length of fine wire. Glue them to the fruit. Wire the trunk of the tree.

ORANGES & LEMONS PURSE

This luxurious circular purse is embroidered to look like slices of fruit and is rich in contrasting textures: use tiny beads to echo the pitted skin and droplets of juice on the flesh.

YOU WILL NEED

MATERIALS
15 cm/6 in pieces velvet or
* brocade, one in orange and*
* one in yellow*
two 15 cm/6 in pieces yellow silk
stranded embroidery thread:
* white, crimson, orange, yellow*
* and lime green*
small glass beads: yellow, orange
* and clear*
12 cm/4¾ in zip
matching sewing thread

EQUIPMENT
scissors
tracing paper
pencil
tailor's chalk
embroidery needle
pins
tacking thread
sewing needle

1 Cut out circles of 14 cm/ 5½ in diameter from each fabric: one of orange velvet, one of yellow velvet, and two of silk for the lining. Copy the template at the back of the book, enlarge to the same size as the circle and transfer the design to the velvet using tailor's chalk.

Embroider a line of chain stitch in white for the pith. On the ruby orange side, sew crimson segments and orange flesh, on the lemon side sew yellow segments and lemon and lime flesh. Use chain stitch for the segments and back stitch for the flesh. Add yellow and orange beads for the pitted skin, and clear beads for drops of moisture. With right sides together, pin and tack the zip in position, leaving a 1 cm/½ in seam allowance.

2 Stitch along both sides of the zip. Open the zip and complete the seam round the rest of the circle.

3 With right sides together, sew the two pieces of lining together halfway round. Turn to the right side. Put the purse, inside out, inside the lining. Turn in the remaining lining seam allowance and slip stitch it to the zip. Turn right way out.

TEMPLATES

To enlarge the templates to the correct size, use either a grid system or a photocopier. For the grid system, trace the template and draw a grid of evenly spaced squares over your tracing. To scale up, draw a larger grid on another piece of paper. Copy the outline on to the second grid by taking each square individually and drawing the relevant part of the outline in the larger square. Finally, draw over the lines to make sure they are continuous.

Oranges & Lemons
Tea Towel p36

Fruit Tree Table Decorations p54

Citrus Roller Blind p22

Pinpricked Fruit
Lampshade p12

Lemon Tiles p30

Lemon Slice Table
Napkin p44

*Sponge-printed Fruit
Shelf-edging p42*

Orange-tree Notebook Cover p16

*Punched Tin Citrus Door Panel
p28*

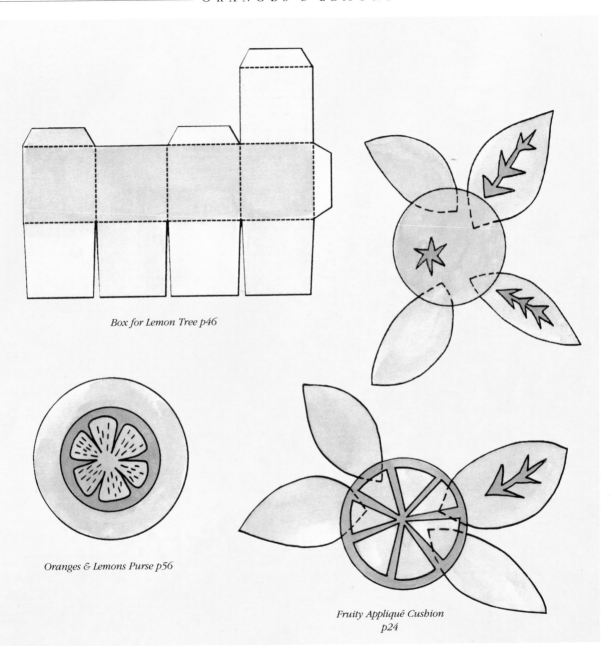

Box for Lemon Tree p46

Oranges & Lemons Purse p56

Fruity Appliqué Cushion
p24

Fruity Bracelet p34

Mexican Painted Citrus Tray p14

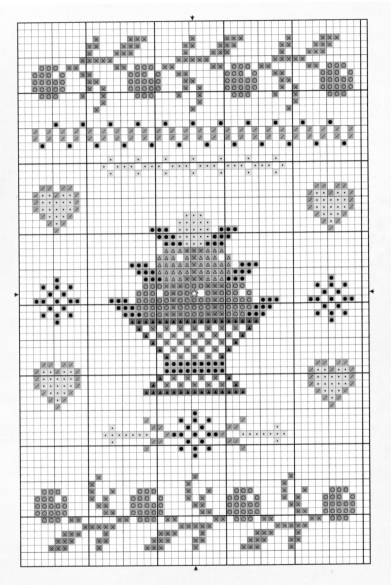

		726	yellow
● ●		832	light olive
		729	ochre
△ △		722	light orange
▲ ▲		801	chocolate brown
○ ○		720	orange
✕ ✕		730	dark olive
☆			Middle point

Orange Basket Sampler p32

ACKNOWLEDGEMENTS

The author and publishers would like to thank the following people for designing the projects in this book:

Penny Boylan

Pinpricked Fruit Lampshade p12
Mexican Painted Citrus Tray p14
Citrus Roller Blind p22
Lemon Tiles p30

Louise Brownlow

Lemon Tree p46
Fruit Tree Table Decorations p54

Sophie Embleton

Fruity Bracelet p34
Oranges & Lemons Purse p56

Lucinda Ganderton

Orange-tree Notebook Cover p16
Orange Bowl p20
Fruity Appliqué Cushion p24
Orange Basket Sampler p32
Sponge-printed Fruit Shelf-edging p42

Emma Petitt

Gilded Fruits Glass Bowl p48

Isabel Stanley

Oranges & Lemons Tea Towel p36

Dorothy Wood

Orange-slice Earrings p18
Punched Tin Citrus Door Panel p28
Salt Dough Fruit Basket p38
Lemon Slice Table Napkin p44
Découpage Lemon Mirror Frame p50

Picture Credits
The Publishers would like to thank the following picture agencies
for permission to reproduce the following pictures:
AKG, London: p10 (top). E.T. Archive, London: p9, p10 (bottom), p11.
Fine Art Photographic: p8.